A FIRST LOOK AT ROCKS

**By Millicent E. Selsam
and Joyce Hunt**

ILLUSTRATED BY HARRIETT SPRINGER

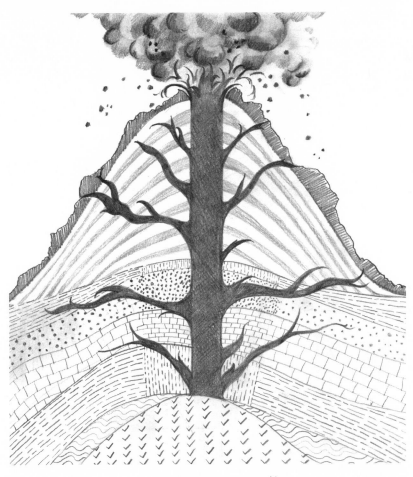

WALKER AND COMPANY ✹ NEW YORK

Library of Congress Cataloging in Publication Data

Selsam, Millicent Ellis, 1912–
   A first look at rocks.

   (A First look at series)
   Includes index.
   Summary: Describes the distinguishing characteristics
of various kinds of rocks.
   1. Petrology—Juvenile literature. [1. Rocks.
2. Petrology] I. Hunt, Joyce. II. Springer, Harriett,
ill. III. Title. IV. Series: Selsam, Millicent Ellis,
1912–   . First look at series.
QE432.2.S35 1984   552   83-40394
ISBN 0-8027-6531-9

First published in the United States of America
in 1984 by the Walker Publishing Company, Inc.
This edition printed in 1986.
Published simultaneously in Canada by John Wiley & Sons
Canada, Limited, Rexdale, Ontario.

ISBN: 0-8027-6531-9 Reinforced

Printed in the United States of America

10   9   8   7   6   5   4   3

A *FIRST LOOK AT* SERIES

Each of the nature books in this series is planned to develop the child's powers of observation—to train him or her to notice distinguishing characteristics. A leaf is a leaf. A bird is a bird. An insect is an insect. That is true. But what makes an oak leaf different from a maple leaf? Why is a hawk different from an eagle, or a beetle different from a bug?

Classification is a painstaking science. These books give a child the essence of the search for differences that is the basis for scientific classification.

The authors wish to thank Professor C. E. Nehru, Department of Geology, American Museum of Natural History, for reading the text of this book and offering many helpful suggestions.

For Brian and Russell

Rocks are everywhere.
They make up mountains and hills.
They are under the soil of forests.
They are under the sand of deserts and
under the water of oceans and rivers.
They are under cities and towns.
The crust of the whole earth is rock.

Here are some rocks.
How do you tell one from another?

There are many things to look for.

Some sparkle.
Some are dull.
Some have speckles.
Some have stripes.
Some have layers.

What a rock looks like depends
on how it was formed.

Deep within the earth
there is hot molten (melted) rock.
Sometimes the molten rock comes up
through the opening of a volcano.
Sometimes the molten rock comes up
through cracks in the earth.
When the molten rock pours out of the earth
it is called *lava*.

When the lava cools it turns solid
and is called *igneous* (IG-nee-us) rock.
Igneous means "made by fire."

IGNEOUS ROCKS

These igneous rocks are speckled
like salt and pepper.

Find the one with large grains.

Find the one with small grains.

GRANITE

THIS ROCK IS OFTEN USED IN BUILDINGS

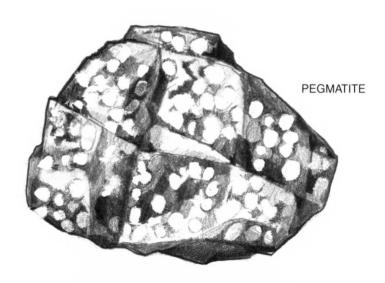

PEGMATITE

ALL THE PRECIOUS STONES IN THE WORLD
COME FROM THIS ROCK.

13

These three igneous rocks are not speckled.
You cannot see any grains.

Obsidian is dark and glassy.
Basalt is dark and dull.
Felsite is light and dull.
Which is which?

Pumice and *Scoria* look like rocky sponges.
They both have holes.

Pumice is so light that it floats on water.

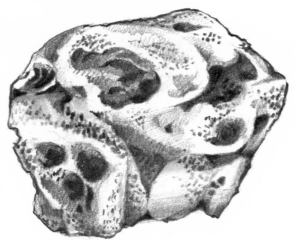

Scoria is darker and heavier than pumice.
It sinks in water.

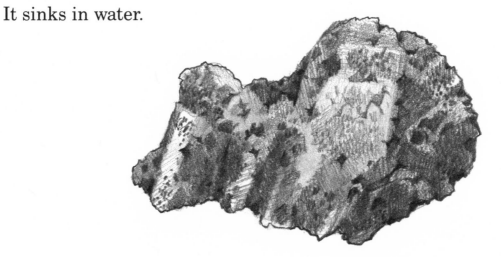

Everywhere on land the wind blows and the rain falls.
This makes rocks crack, break and crumble.
Bits and pieces of the rock tumble down into streams.
The streams carry them to the rivers
and the rivers carry them to the sea.

The bits and pieces can be as small as sand grains
or as big as pebbles.
These are called *sediments*.
Millions of tons of these sediments pile up
layer upon layer.
The top layers press down on the lower layers.
Over millions of years, the sediment
becomes *sedimentary* (sed-i-MEN-ta-ree) rock.

RAIN

STREAM

RIVER

SEA

SEDIMENT

17

SEDIMENTARY ROCK

Shale is sedimentary rock that comes from mud or clay.
The grains are so fine you can hardly see them.
Find the shale.

Sandstone is the sedimentary rock that comes from sand.
The grains are large enough to see.
Find the sandstone.

Conglomerate (con-GLOM-er-ate) or pudding stone
is made up of large rounded pebbles.
Find the conglomerate.

Breccia (BRECH-ee-yuh) is made up of large sharp-edged
pieces of rock.
Find the breccia.

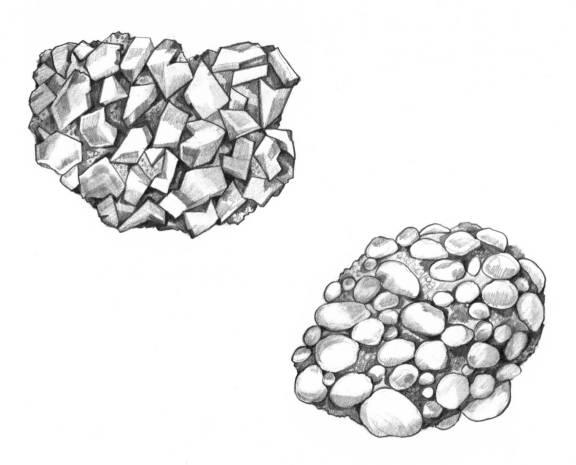

19

Sometimes sedimentary rocks are formed
from the crushed shells of tiny sea animals
that pile up just the way the sand and pebbles do.
You can see the shells in this limestone rock.

Sometimes limestone is not formed from sea animals
but from the chemical lime in the sea.
You can't see any shells in this limestone rock.

Very often limestone is white and
looks like lump sugar.

The Grand Canyon is made up of layers of
shale, sandstone, and limestone.
These sedimentary rocks were deposited millions of years ago
when this land was covered by the sea.
The sea dried up.

Then the Colorado River cut its way through
the layers of rock and made the canyon.
Even today, bits and pieces of rock are
crumbling and falling into the river.

The earth is four and a half billion years old
and is always changing.

Mountains rise up.

Seas dry out.

Continents move.

Earthquakes shake the earth.

Volcanoes erupt.

As a result of all this, some rocks get buried
deep in the earth where it is very hot.
The heat bakes and changes the buried rock
the way heat in an oven bakes and changes dough into bread.
There is also great pressure on the buried rock
from the weight of the rock above.
This pressure also changes the buried rock.
Changed rock is called *metamorphic* (metta-MOR-fik) rock.
"Meta" means change and "morphic" means form.

METAMORPHIC ROCK

Each kind of igneous and sedimentary rock
changes into its own kind of metamorphic rock.
The metamorphic rock is usually harder
than the rock it comes from.

granite
speckled

changes into

gneiss (nice)
striped

shale
dull, soft,
and sometimes
crumbly.

changes into

slate
shiny, hard, splits into sheets

limestone
small, dull grains

changes into

marble
large grains that sparkle

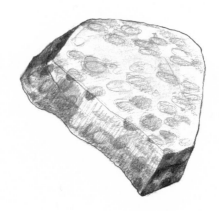

sandstone
easy to break,
rough and gritty.

changes into

quartzite
hard to break,
smooth and shiny.

27

In this map of North
America, you can see
where the three main
kinds of rock are.

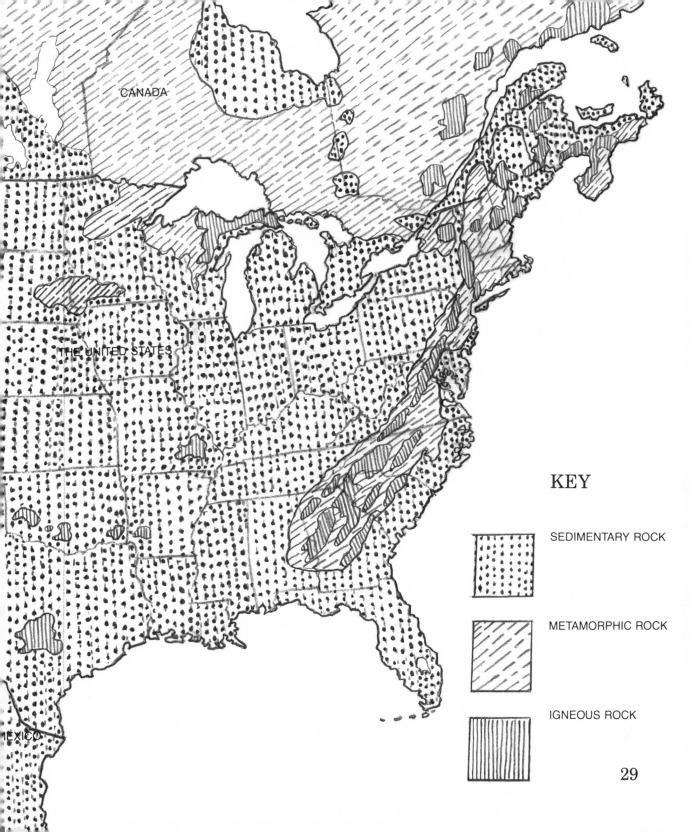

CANADA

THE UNITED STATES

MEXICO

KEY

SEDIMENTARY ROCK

METAMORPHIC ROCK

IGNEOUS ROCK

29

To tell rocks apart:

Look for speckles or stripes.

Look for dark or light rocks.

 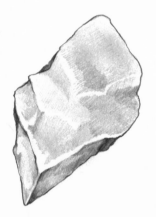

Look for glassy rocks.

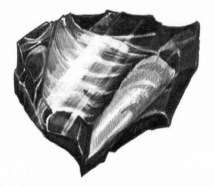

Look for rocks with holes.

Look for rocks with small grains or pebbles.

Look for rocks with pieces of shell.

Look for rocks that split into sheets.

ROCKS IN THIS BOOK